HARRY
BENSON'S
PEOPLE

HARRY BENSON'S PEOPLE

MAINSTREAM
PUBLISHING

First published in Great Britain 1990 by
MAINSTREAM PUBLISHING COMPANY (EDINBURGH) LTD
7 Albany Street
Edinburgh EH1 3UG

ISBN 1 85158 322 X (cloth)
ISBN 1 85158 370 X (paper)

British Library Cataloguing in Publication Data

Benson, Harry
Harry Benson's people.
I. Title
779.0942

Typeset in Garamond by Novatext Graphix, Edinburgh
Printed and Bound in Great Britain by Butler & Tanner Ltd, Frome
Design and Layout by Wide Art, Edinburgh and Gigi Benson, New York

To Gigi, Tessa and Wendy

CONTENTS

ACKNOWLEDGMENTS

To BE a photojournalist you have to have a picture editor who likes your work and will give you the important assignments. Three people come to mind: M. C. Marden of *People*, John Loengard of *Life* and Mary Dunn of *Time*. Without their encouragement I wouldn't have a career, let alone a book. I also owe a special thanks to some editors: Dick Stolley, who is the editor I've worked with the longest in my career; Lanny Jones of *People*; and Jim Gaines of *Life*. It has also been a privilege working alongside the greats in photography like Alfred Eisenstaedt. I must mention David Friend of *Life* and Dave Sherman who gave me my first assignment with this magazine, my first foot in the door; Gunn Brinson of the London *Sunday Times Magazine*; Sam Kusumoto and John Jonny of *Minolta;* Lord Beaverbrook, proprietor of the *Daily Express*; Derek Marks, editor, and Frank Spooner, picture editor, of the *Express* when I came to America with the Beatles; Charlie McBain of the *Hamilton Advertiser* and Tommy Fitzpatrick and Ian Buchan of the Glasgow *Evening Times*. I would also like to thank my assistant of several years, Jon Delano, who I'm sure has a story or two to tell himself. And to Mary Sue Morris, Lynn Crystal, Mary Lou Davis, Joyce MacRae and Tom Hawkyard for organising my photo exhibits, and especially to Jackie Lacey of Christie's Glasgow and Bill Campbell of Mainstream Publishing for making this book a reality. And last I would like to thank my mother in Clarkston for never doubting and always encouraging me.

O WAD SOME POWER THE GIFTIE GIE US
TO SEE OURSELS AS ITHERS SEE US!

Robert Burns

Harry directing the Reagans in the White House for the 'kiss' photograph.

FOREWORD

by
Richard B. Stolley

SOMEBODY once said that the secret of photojournalism is F-8 and be there. Harry Benson is a great photojournalist because he does seem to know one F-stop from another but, far more important, he is always there. And 'there' means being at the right place at the right time with the right equipment and the right reflexes and the subject (if there is one) in the right mood.

Harry and I have been working together for more than twenty years. I ran a doubletruck of his (the Vietnam peacetalks in Paris) in the last issue of the weekly *Life* magazine which I edited in December 1972; I ran his lead article on Palm Beach in the first issue of *People* magazine in February 1974, and for the eight years I was managing editor of *People* and the three years I was managing editor of the monthly *Life*, I ran more Harry Benson stories than you could shake a stick at.

To tell the truth, there were times when I felt like shaking that stick at Harry. He is an artist, and a driven one at that, and like so many members of that elite society, he can be exasperating. On assignment, Harry is so single-minded in his pursuit of the story that he is sometimes painfully oblivious to the feelings of the reporters he is working with. He once peevishly drove off and left a young woman on a Pennsylvania roadside because he was sure she had mixed up directions.

Harry can also be a trial for editors. Long ago I learned that the flip side of Harry's artistic drive is a mild paranoia. To send him off on assignment is to insure a barrage of anxious phone calls about progress, problems, the subject, the reporter, the weather, highway conditions, something, anything. The purpose of these plaintive conversations is to clear Harry's cerebral passages, and it's a small price to pay for the pictures you know he's going to bring back.

The images in this book represent Harry Benson at the top of his canny and elegant form. To get them he had to play a variety of roles: diplomat, negotiator, wheedler, compromiser, and only then, photographer. Harry is like a skilled actor; he uses his whole body on the job. He bobs and weaves, dashes a hand through his curly thatch of hair, beams a boyish grin, pleads and cajoles in a beguiling Scottish accent, tells gently indiscreet stories about famous people he has photographed so as to put the present subject at ease. The technique almost always succeeds. (But if, once in a while, Harry is balked by a subject or competitor or even colleague, the miscreant is branded with the ultimate Benson epithet: 'A nasty piece of work!')

Some of these pictures bring back vivid personal memories. Who else but Harry Benson could have put up with Bobby Fischer, the brilliant but totally impossible chess master, for weeks in Iceland – and still get him on to the tundra to be nuzzled by a sympathetic horse? After *Life* concluded delicate negotiations with the Kennedy family for a picture of Caroline and John Jr together, the first they had ever posed for, the photographer, to make them feel comfortable for a loving brother-sister portrait, was clearly Benson.

When all the stars gathered to record 'We are the World', Benson was the man who would never be intimidated by that battalion of egos. And when Harry saw the bright red bath-tub in Willie Nelson's Colorado hideaway, it was only a matter of time before he had the singer and his wife, Connie, under the bubbles.

Other photographers have energy and an eye; Harry augments both with an editorial sense, a virtue unfortunately rare among some of his competitors. He knows that stories have a beginning, middle and end, and he knows how to document each. He once wrote: 'No matter how mundane the assignment may be, there is always one good picture to be taken, and possibly a great one.' In this book, Harry Benson shows you some good pictures, many great pictures and more than a few extraordinary pictures. It is by those that I judge Harry, and treasure him.

Richard B Stolley
Editorial Director, *Time* Inc Magazines
New York, May 1990

John and Jackie Kennedy came to London in the summer of 1961, after he
became President. London and Paris belonged to Jackie – the press couldn't get
enough of her. I must have stood outside her sister Lee Radziwill's house for six
or seven hours, for it was late in the afternoon when Jackie stepped out to give
the waiting photographers a picture.

One afternoon in 1956 I was walking around the Botanic Gardens looking for a picture for the *Sketch*. I happened upon some Glasgow boys up to some mischief. They were cooling off in the Glasgow heatwave although the temperature was no more than seventy-five degrees.

INTRODUCTION

To HAVE an air around my photographs, a space between me and my subjects, is what I like. It's the way I like to work all the time. I don't have a traditional approach. That's why I don't agree with a lot of photographers holding and controlling – there's no air. Trying to control and impose limits on what is happening stifles a photograph. Give the subject air – a freedom – on the off-chance that something spontaneous and natural, something you hoped for, will happen. Something spontaneous is what I always hope for in a photograph. Not trying to hide my presence, I want the whole situation to move, to give the subject some room. Either nothing happens or something wonderful will happen. I don't want my subjects to be made of wood or granite. Photography has got to be fun, it has to be. Why should I try to take photographs like another photographer?

Since I started taking pictures, the content has always been much more important to me than having the sharpest focus or best lighting. Getting the picture is what I want. It's the subject-matter, the content, that counts. 'But what does it mean?' are the words I hear, is the question I've asked all my life in photography. To me a photograph must give information. I like to have information in my photographs. If there is no information, after a time the picture is no longer valid. Pictures I like to take say, 'This was the time, this was the place, I was there.' It doesn't always happen. It's awful when it doesn't.

The problem, the trouble I have with pictures is that afterwards sometimes they embarrass me. I feel really embarrassed by a picture with no wit or edge. A photograph must have a wit and an edge, when you get the better of the subject and get something unexpected, something different.

When I take a picture, sometimes it's very hard to move and other times – not all that often – things get going very well, everything is there on a high level of energy. I'm in another area, on another plane, and it's a wonderful feeling. I push that moment as long as I can to make sure I've taken everything out of the situation, as far as I can go and back again.

Sometimes I have to work very quickly. If I'm not starting to show

Photography in Glasgow in the Fifties was a lot of fun and very, very competitive.
There were an awful lot of good photographers around. It was very hard to get a job.
This photograph was taken in 1957 at Daley's Department Store in Glasgow for the
Daily Sketch when the trapeze-style dress first appeared. The picture was taken with an
MPP, a British copy of the Speed Graphic plate camera.

signs of getting people moving in the first ten minutes, I've got problems. Usually I'm a stranger working in the subject's territory, their home, their office, their familiar ground. If I'm not careful, I can lose it, the momentum. But if I can get myself moving, I can usually get the subject moving. My photography is schizophrenic, dissociated – I don't like to make people too important. A lot of photographers are overawed by their subjects, after all we are keeping their image alive.

Opportunity comes up in photography like an express train, and you've just got to catch it. Looking back on some assignments, I missed it and wish I could go back and photograph them again. Not the Beatles, I feel I photographed them well, even though at the time they were being touted by some as just a flash in the pan, a six-month wonder.

A good picture is obvious, it speaks for itself. It's not a secret. Either you like it or you don't . . .

Photography for me was a godsend. I really don't know what I would have done if photography hadn't been invented. Having to leave

Lord Beaverbrook, proprietor of the London *Daily Express* when I worked there, was the most important person in my journalistic life. I thought he was terrific, the greatest of the press lords. Here he is being given an eighty-fifth birthday party at the Savoy Hotel by another Canadian newspaperman, Lord Thompson of Fleet.

school at fifteen or having to repeat the same grade for the third time were my choices. It was obvious that traditional schooling was not for me. I fared better at the Glasgow School of Art.

My father gave me a box camera, a Coronet Cub, for Christmas when I was eleven years old. My first published picture of a roe deer was taken in Calder Park Zoo, which was founded by my father. It was published in the Glasgow *Evening Times* and I sat and looked at that picture for hours. I can't remember if they paid me for using it, but that wasn't important. Seeing the picture in print was what mattered. That feeling has never left me.

When I was in the Royal Air Force I tried to join a camera club on the base in Bedfordshire. Submitting my photographs to the committee that ran the club, I was told my pictures were not up to standard. Looking back, they were probably right because the pictures were only of things that interested me – football players and dogs. I find it so depressing to remind myself of all this.

There is an energy in these women, these Glasgow housewives, greeting American sailors from a submarine carrying Polaris missiles when they docked in Glasgow in 1961. There had been a controversy over whether or not the sub should be based in Glasgow, but these women didn't seem concerned. They were giving the sailors an enthusiastic welcome.

English schoolboy, David Field, couldn't afford the plane ticket when his class
went on a school trip to Norway in 1962. The plane crashed, killing all his
classmates. I went to his home outside London to photograph him the morning
after. His parents had sent him fishing to take his mind off the tragedy. He
seemed so isolated, so alone.

Prince Phillip, Duke of Edinburgh, had just been made Chancellor of Edinburgh
University. The ceremony became a riotous affair, with the students showing
their appreciation by throwing toilet paper and flour at him. This picture helped
me win a British Press Photographer of the Year award in 1957.
When I asked the *Daily Mail* office to develop the film for me (my paper, the
Sketch, was part of the same newspaper group), I made the mistake of telling
them I had a picture of the toilet paper flying through the air, which their
photographer had missed. When the plate went into the developer, the printer
turned on the light in the darkroom. As a result, this picture is only half the
frame; the other half was fogged – deliberately.

In 1957 HRH Queen Elizabeth II came to Scotland for an official function, to open a
coal mine. She dressed for the occasion.

The Beatles. Paris, France, 1964
They were all just young kids, not really knowing what was happening. It was all happening so fast. We were in John Lennon's room in the George V Hotel. They couldn't go out because they would be mobbed. It was three in the morning when Brian Epstein rang to say 'I Want to Hold Your Hand' was Number One in America and they would be going there to appear on the Ed Sullivan Show. They were elated. I had seen them have pillow fights before, but the exuberance of this one almost became violent at times.

When I tried to get a job on the Glasgow *Evening Citizen*, the picture editor told me I should be feeding animals in my father's zoo. I hated that man when I left his office. Criticism like that knocks you right off balance for a long time.

My first newspaper job which was really my beginning in journalism was for the *Hamilton Advertiser*, the largest local weekly in Scotland. Four years under editor Tom Murray was the equivalent of a university education. Some days I took the train to London trying to get a job on Fleet Street, then the home of the British press. My colleague at the *Advertiser* and my friend today, Charlie McBain, used to cover for me and do my work while I went walking around Fleet Street with my portfolio. On about my seventh trip, I finally got to see the assistant picture editor of the *Daily Sketch,* Freddy Wackett. I could tell, I got the feeling, that he was slightly impressed. On the way out I asked if there was a chance, and he gave me a little nod. Within two years of covering Scotland for the *Sketch*, I moved to London, working later for *Queen* magazine and the *Daily Express.* When I came to America with the Beatles on their first tour I knew I would never go back.

I'm just as keen now as when I started out, just as apprehensive, just as insecure, just as excited at the prospect of taking pictures that hopefully people will want to look at. I like the challenge of not knowing what lies ahead.

One minute I'm on the second floor of the White House; in a few hours I'm working on a cover photograph in the studio. It's a little like changing channels on the television set. I have to be able to switch channels, to switch emotional channels quickly.

It's an adventure to record the lives of important, intelligent or famous people and if they are all three, better yet. To give an honest impression, to get people to let their guard down so that I can photograph what they usually like to keep hidden, to capture a moment that won't be repeated, to take that one photograph worth looking at, is what I want to do.

Harry in the studio with Brooke Shields and model, Kay Zunker.

Princess Caroline of Monaco. Monte Carlo, Monaco, 1986
Having preconceived notions and expecting some kind of flighty jet-setter, I was pleasantly surprised by her gracious, sensitive manner. She is a patron of the Royal Ballet of Monaco which was a favourite of her mother's.

27

Caroline Kennedy.
Hyannis Port, Massachusetts, 1986
A very happy wedding day with the whole family in
attendance, she was given away by her Uncle Ted. Her
mother was nervous and Caroline was making the most
of her day. Of all the photographs I took that day
Caroline, her mother and I all liked this one the best.

Alexander Solzhenitsyn. Vermont, 1981
It was the first time in his eight years of exile from
Russia that anyone had been allowed to photograph
him at his home. I asked him what he liked about
his adopted country, and he said the air smelled
free in America.

30

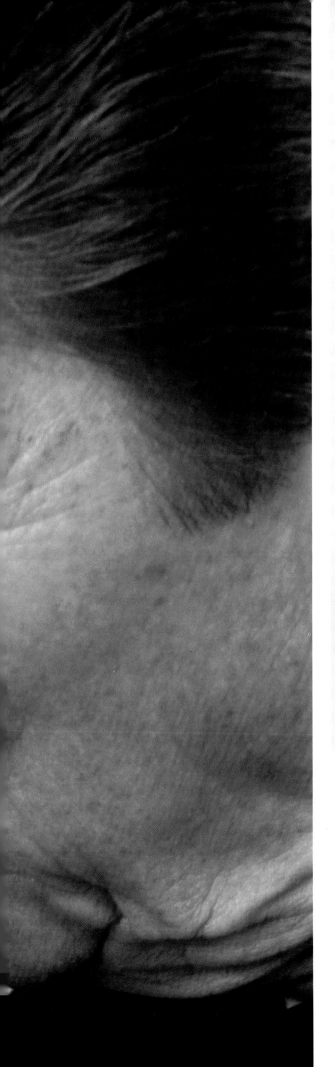

President and Mrs Ronald Reagan. The White House, Washington DC, 1985

It was apparent that theirs was a genuine love story. I wanted to show it in the form of the big-screen kiss at the fade out of a Hollywood film. When *Vanity Fair* asked me to photograph them in the White House, I got my chance, but only for six minutes. In a small room off the main ballroom on the night of a state dinner they were to stop off for a quick photograph. When they arrived I put on a tape of Sinatra singing 'Nancy with the Laughing Face'. They smiled and started dancing.

**HRH Prince and Princess
Michael of Kent. London, 1986**
They were in their bedroom in
Kensington Palace. The Princess
told the Prince to try not to look
stupid for the photograph.
Afterwards I found it
embarrassing to look at or speak
to him. Sometimes you find
people are like what you have
been told about them. She wanted
to edit and choose the
photographs, telling me that was
the Royal way. I explained that I
was not a Royal photographer.

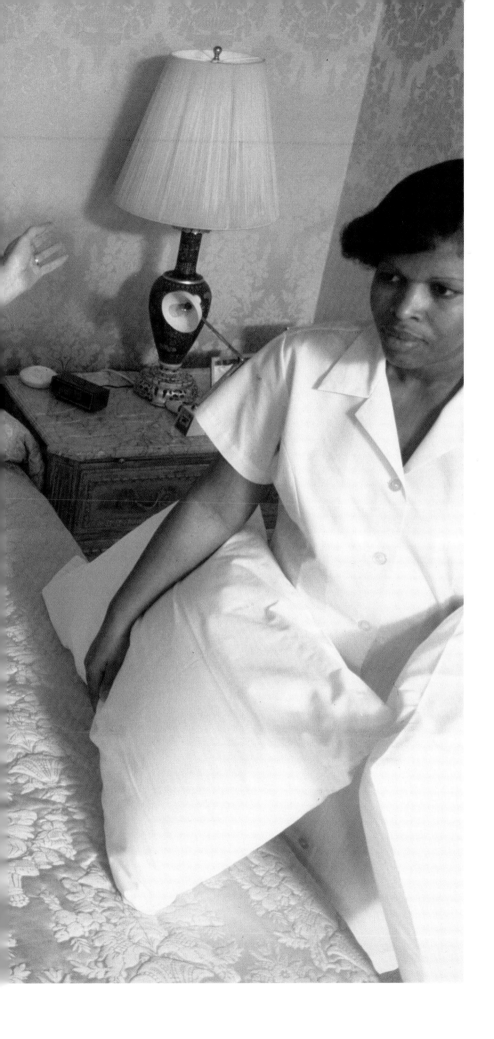

Leona Helmsley. New York, 1984
She enjoyed being queen of her hotels. She relished the power. She liked to walk down the corridors telling any of her employees in passing who she was and what to do – dust the table, empty the ashtray.

Jim and Tammy Bakker. Malibu, 1987
I wanted to photograph them near the water at the
beach-house they had rented shortly after his trouble
with the PTL (Praise the Lord) Ministry began.
Working them down to the water's edge I heard
someone from the house shout, 'Don't go any further,
you'll get your feet wet.' I sent my assistant, Jon
Delano, to tell that person to keep quiet. The water
eventually came up around their feet. Tammy told me
she was worried that in the heat her mascara would
melt. He was smaller and she was larger than I had
expected. If anything, they were bewildered by the
situation they were in – being accused of diverting
funds from the PTL for their personal use and having a
secretary accuse Jim of asking for sexual favours with
hush money thrown in.

Marine Lt-Col Oliver North. Washington DC, 1987
He completely believed that what he had done in the Iran-contra affair was
right. Fifty-five million television viewers watched as he explained why he
believed the US was right in selling arms to Iran and in using the money to aid
the Nicaraguan contras. Very self-righteously he also told me none of the men
under him in Vietnam had ever smoked any dope. Some people thought he was
an American hero, a man who would go through fire and brimstone in his fight
against what he felt was a Communist threat.

Soldiers. Near Bonn, West Germany, 1982
American soldiers on manoeuvres, simulating an invasion using chemical warfare.

Berlin Wall. West Berlin, 1982
On a Saturday night in a café near Checkpoint Charlie I came across a West Berlin street gang, while doing a story for *Life* on West German youth. The next day they showed up at the Wall and I started taking pictures. One pulled out a gun, another a knife. I was startled to see all the weapons they had.

FOLLOWING PAGE

USA for Africa. Los Angeles, 1985
It took all night when America's biggest rock stars came together to record 'We Are the World' to raise money to feed the hungry in Africa. Quincey Jones, the musical director, posted a sign at the entrance of the recording studio which said, 'Leave your ego outside' — and they did. It was fun watching some of them trying very hard to be humble.

Somalia refugee camp with Dr Eric Avery. Las Dhure, 1981
Thousands arrive daily from war-torn Ethiopia to the refugee camps set up in Somalia. The chanting and moaning of the starving children never stop.

President Daniel Ortega. Managua, Nicaragua, 1986
Hearing he was a big baseball fan, I brought down a New York Mets tee-shirt
and cap which delighted him. Catching him just as he finished jogging, his rifle
never left his side. That night I got a call asking if the entire family could be
photographed. Explaining that my plane left at nine the next morning, I was
told to be there at seven. Explaining that airport security would take longer, Mrs
Ortega laughed and said, 'We'll take care of that.' Leaving, I had a military
escort right up to the plane.

President Ferdinand and Imelda Marcos. Manila, Philippines, 1985
His palace was surrounded by slums but inside it was very luxurious with huge
paintings and ornate thrones. He told me people said he was a fanatic but the
only thing he was fanatical about was his health. I wanted to show the strong
man keeping fit.

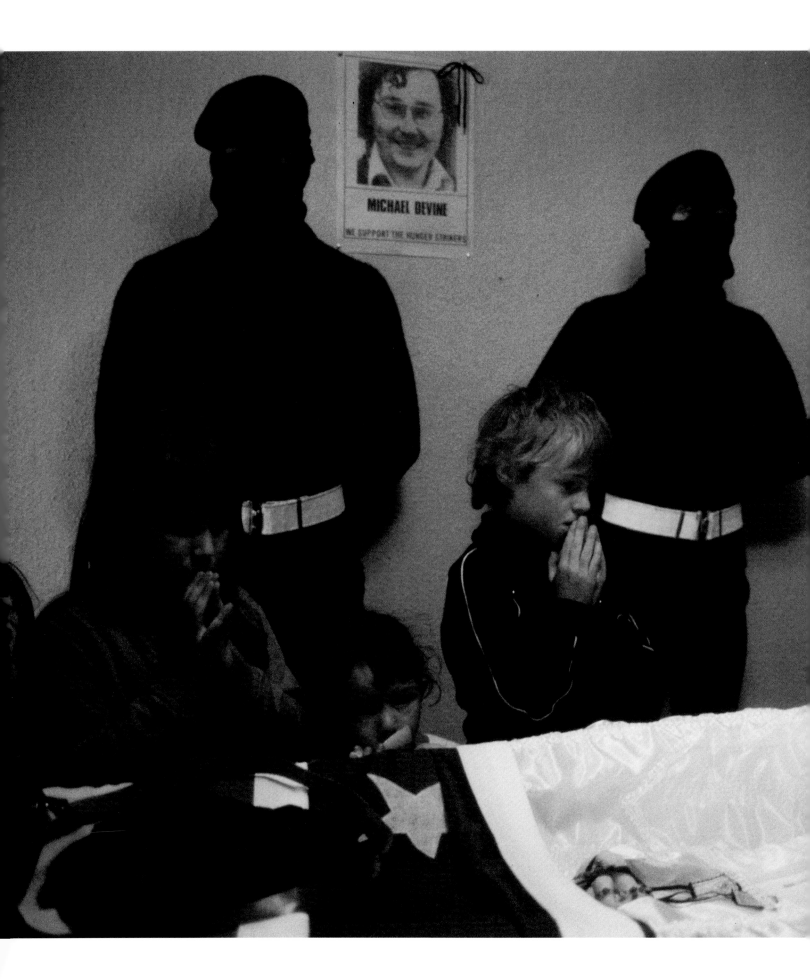

Mickey Devine. Londonderry, 1981
He was the last of the IRA hunger-strikers to die. I'd
never been to an Irish wake before and in the room
adjacent to where he lay were tea, cake and sandwiches.
All the neighbours would come in to have something
to eat and pay their respects. It was incongruous to see
in the room beside the body masked IRA soldiers with
machine guns while 200 yards down the road were
British Army patrols.

IRA soldiers. Northern Ireland, 1985
A group of IRA members on the way back from
manoeuvres rested in the late afternoon. In order to get
to where they were, I had to agree to be blindfolded.

**Shooting Gallery.
New York, 1980**
Doing a story for *Life* on teenage
drug abuse, I was photographing
in a 'shooting gallery', an
abandoned building where
addicts go to shoot up, when the
police raided the place. They were
as surprised to see me as I was to
see them. Sadly, these kids have
probably all died of AIDS because
they were passing the same needle
from one to the other
indiscriminately.

William F. Buckley, Jr. New York, 1988
There was something very sensous about this
couch, not a word that normally springs to mind
when you think of a conservative Republican. It
reminded me of the Victorian era when people
presented a very proper appearance to the outside
world but their private lives were luxurious,
almost to the point of decadence.

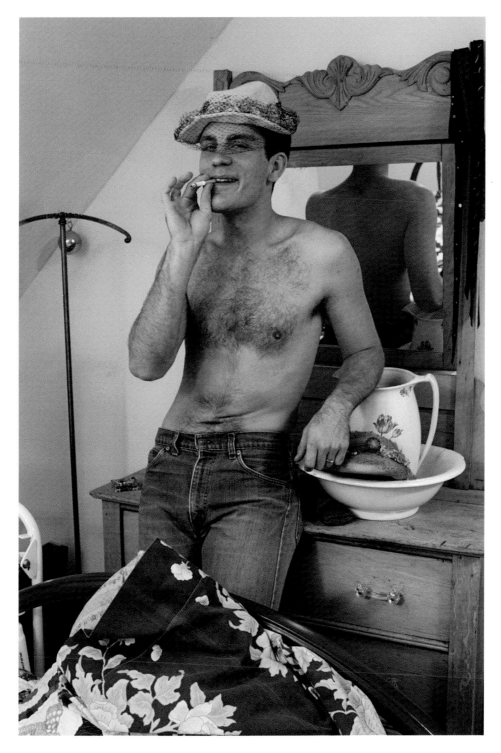

John Malkovich. Chicago, 1984

He was being touted in a press release as 'The New Bogart' and I was sent to see
for myself. I didn't think he looked or acted in the least like Bogart. He was
intelligent and accommodating, but what amazed me were his crooked teeth.

William Hurt. Los Angeles, 1987

He likes to go salmon fishing in Scotland. He had just won the Academy Award
for Best Actor and was filming James Brooks' *Broadcast News*. I kept calling
him John instead of William, and he told me not to·worry, everyone did that
all the time.

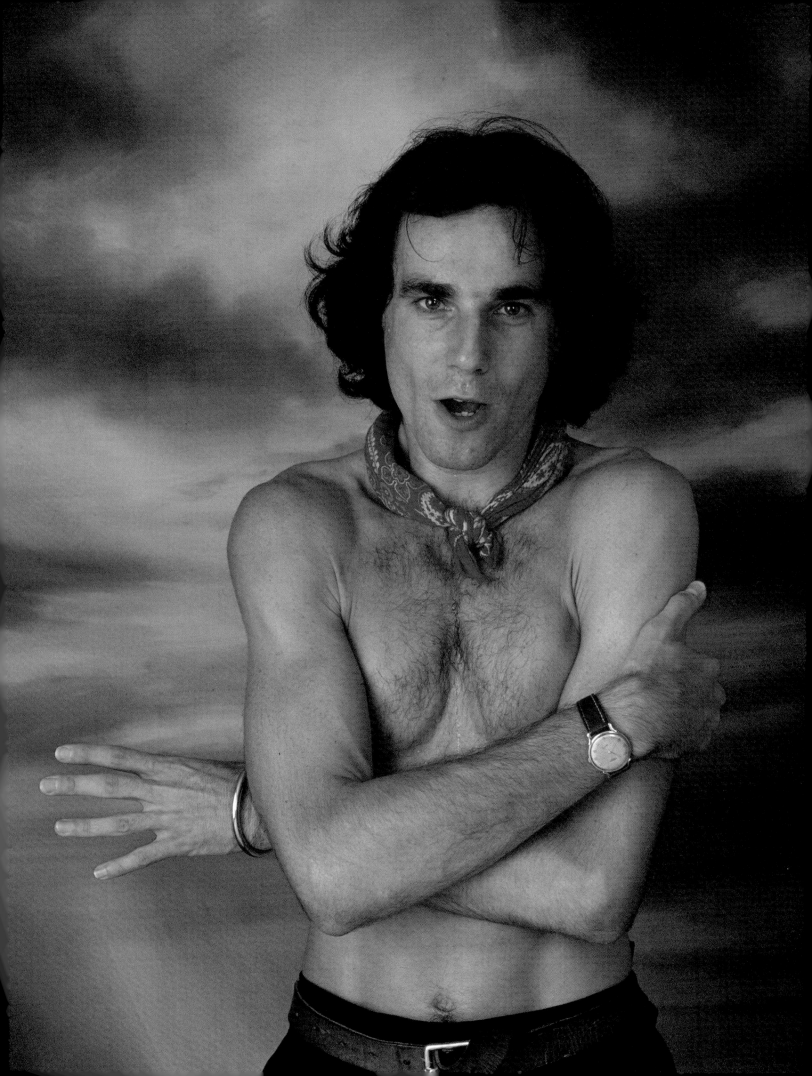

Matthew Broderick. New York, 1983
He was appearing in a play at the time and his first hit film, *War Games*
had just come out. I asked him what he liked to do for relaxation and
this is what I got.

Daniel Day Lewis. New York, 1989
He was very accessible and open. His tremendous success has not made him close
off to people yet. He was more interested in talking about soccer than acting. He
wasn't thinking about his image – in other words, he was an actor, sure of
himself. Shortly after this photograph was taken he won the Oscar for Best Actor.

Christian LaCroix. New York, 1987
Surrounded by models and ladies after his première collection was shown in
New York. A fashion show is like a Broadway opening night, especially if it's a
hit. This opening was a hit.

Yves St Laurent. Paris, France, 1977
Backstage at his collection, St Laurent nervously oversees every last detail before
each model steps out on the walkway. An urgency is there, every moment
counts, everything goes very quickly.

Leonard and Allison Stern. New York, 1989
Allison playfully coaxes her husband, Leonard, from the sofa in their art-filled
Fifth Avenue townhouse. She is an Emmy Award-winning television
documentary producer and devotes much of her time to the causes of Central
Park Zoo while he oversees his publishing and the Hartz Mountain pet-food
empire. In conversation, Allison is one of the few busy people who really seem to
listen when someone else is talking.

Valentino. Rome, 1987
In his design studio in Rome, he was preparing a collection. He said he worked
so hard designing beautiful clothes so that he could enjoy seeing beautiful ladies
wearing them.

Margaret Trudeau Kemper and son Kyle. Ottowa, Ontario, Canada, 1988
Now remarried and a housewife who cooks and plants in her garden . . . To
think, a few years ago the former First Lady of Canada was driving her husband
crazy with her antics.

Fawn Hall. Annandale, 1987
Oliver North's loyal secretary who had to testify during the Iran-Contra
hearings. I wanted to show her as a fawn, running through the woods.

Cindy Lauper. New York, 1984.
Rock singer Lauper had once paid a visit to London and
I think she never got any further than the King's Road.

69

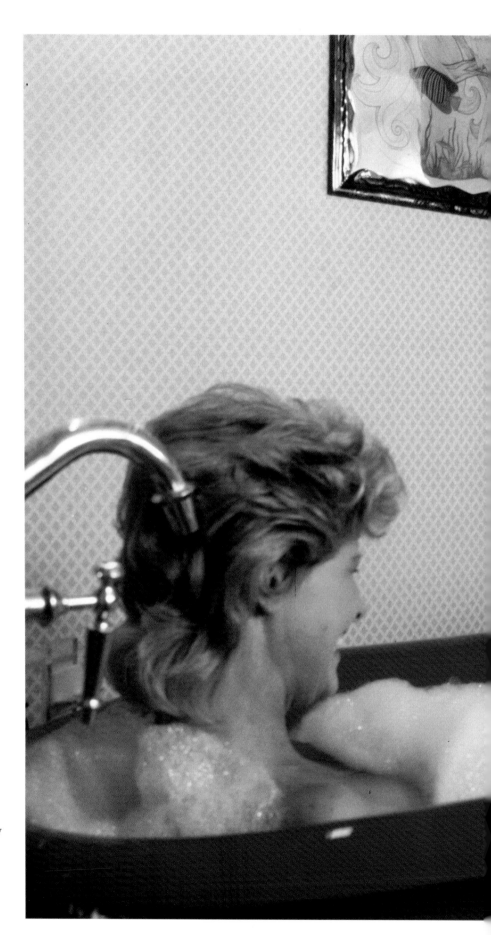

**Willie and Connie Nelson.
Evergreen, Colorado, 1983**
Wife Connie was happy to oblige when I suggested they
take a bubble bath together. She wanted his fans to see
she was number one in Willie's life.

70

Daryl Hannah. New York, 1989

I remember having to wait about four hours for her to have her hair and make-up done on a very hot September day. We had never met before, and she had very little to say. In the empty living-room of her new apartment I asked her to lean against the mirror over the fireplace and noticed the soles of her feet were dirty. I always hope that something unexpected, out of my control, will happen.

Sonia Braga. New York, 1988

She had just filmed *The Milagro Beanfield War* when she came into my studio — this petite woman with great long hair. What else could I do?

Fred and Robyn Astaire.
Los Angeles, 1981
When I asked him to dance, he said
he would, then he wouldn't. The
closest I got was when he crossed
his legs in the recognisable Astaire
pose. A very elegant man.

Francis Bacon. New York, 1975
Overseeing the hanging of his work at the Metropolitan Museum of Art, he
rested for just a moment. Afterwards we went around to some bars in the
Bowery.

Sammy Davis Jr. Los Angeles, 1990
I photographed him when he opened in London in 1959 at the Pigalle and have
never, then or now, seen an entertainer like him – one who could do so much.
While photographing him recently, I reminded him of our earlier meeting. He
had recently been operated on for throat cancer. He was a small man and I was
shocked to see just how small he had become.

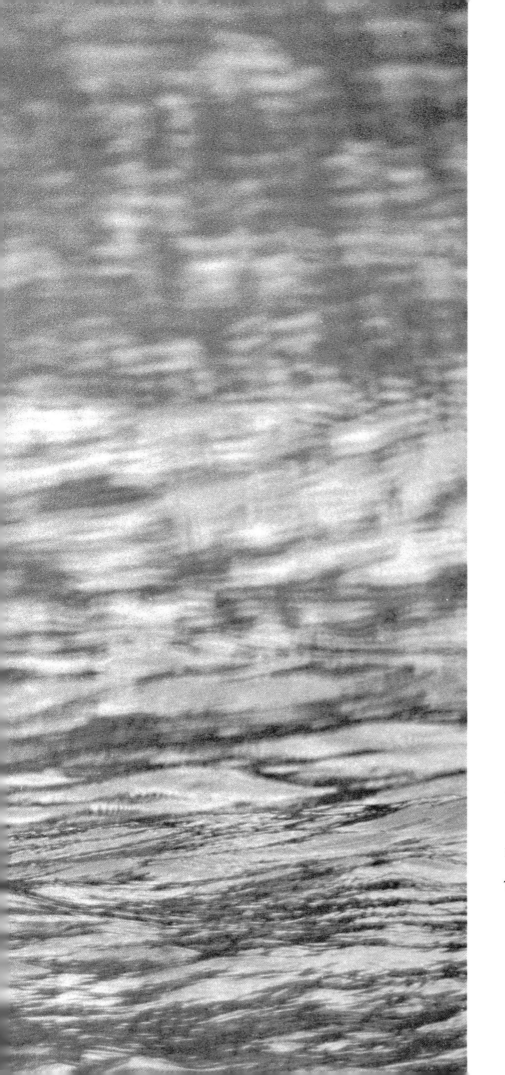

Greta Garbo. Antigua, 1976
As a child I heard my mother and father talking about the 'great Garbo'. When she looked straight at me without her sunglasses on, I wasn't going to let the chance pass. Staking out some one like Garbo on the beach can be fun, but most of all it keeps me honest. It really means I haven't forgotten how I started out. There is strategy and cunning involved, working alone, not sharing any information with colleagues. It's a loner's business, photojournalism. It is not a team sport.

Mrs Ethel Kennedy. Los Angeles, 1968
After Robert Kennedy was shot, there was hysteria and chaos. The noise was
deafening. There had been all that happiness at the beginning of the evening.
When Mrs Kennedy was taken to his side, she cried, 'Give him air.' At times I
still can't believe I was beside him at the end of his life. I liked Bobby.
I kept thinking, he'd understand how important this is, recording
history, doing my job.

Coretta Scott King and Children. Atlanta, 1968
Mrs King and her children were getting off the plane that carried her husband's
body back to Atlanta for burial. They all came together in the doorway for
just a moment.

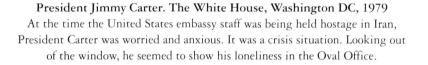

President Jimmy Carter. The White House, Washington DC, 1979
At the time the United States embassy staff was being held hostage in Iran,
President Carter was worried and anxious. It was a crisis situation. Looking out
of the window, he seemed to show his loneliness in the Oval Office.

Yves Montand. St Paul de Vence, France, 1987
Our appointment was set for nine in the morning and I had travelled all night
from New York to get there. We were both having breakfast, separately, at La
Colombe d'Or. At five to nine he left and I could see he was getting into a car
outside. I rushed out. He thought I wanted his autograph. He had forgotten our
appointment and was very apologetic. Later he told me that Simone Signoret,
who had recently died, had been the love of his life.

Sir Winston Churchill.
Harrow School, England, 1965
It was Sir Winston's last visit to his old school, Harrow.
He went back each year at Christmas. The students
cheered and sang out, 'And Churchill's name shall win
acclaim through each new generation.'

Rob Lowe. Los Angeles, 1990
Driving along, he honked the horn and waved at any pretty girls we passed. At the pier at Santa Monica we stopped. He told me he had gone to school nearby. I liked his openness and honesty about the ups and downs of his career.

Norman Parkinson. Tobago, 1983
We had known each other since the Fifties, working on *Queen* magazine. He was a photographer who understood what I meant when I said, 'Let's do something outrageous and fun.' He showed me his wardrobe. I chose the long kaftan and pith helmet and we were off to the beach near his home. The movement and fun in some ways tell you more than if he were standing still, looking straight into the camera.

Tracy Ullman. Los Angeles, 1987
She is a big hit in Hollywood. When she heard my
voice she said, 'You're from Glasgow.' She said she
loved Glasgow and had worked there for the BBC.
Again, something beyond my control that was amusing
happened. As she was posing, her Yorkshire terrier had
a pee on her foot. A very funny lady in person as well as
on television.

Goldie Hawn. Los Angeles, 1975
She had just completed the film *Shampoo* when this photograph was taken and
she just climbed up the tree of her own accord. She seemed to have fun that day.

Betsey Johnson. New York, 1982
One of New York's best off-beat fashion designers for over twenty years, she
seems to thrive amid the chaos of the renovation of her design studio.

The Who. Vancouver, British Columbia, 1980
People warned me to be careful with Pete Townsend, that he was difficult and
had a history of being impossible. I found him to be very cooperative to the
point of giving orders that I could roam around and even go on stage during a
performance.

Dennis Quaid. New York, 1984
The Right Stuff had just come out. It was his first major film and he portrayed an
astronaut. He talked incessantly and I kept calling him Randy, which was his
brother's name. He laughed and said it didn't matter. He keeps fit by boxing
and said an actor must know how to move. So I asked him to move.

Gilda Radner. New York, 1977
It was not hard to take a funny picture of Gilda Radner. She was a funny lady
who told me that when she danced, in her mind she became Rita Hayworth.

Mrs Betty Ford. Alexandria, Virginia, 1974
Knowing she had wanted to be a model when she was younger meant she
probably knew how to have fun with the camera so I asked Mrs Ford to lie down
in the grass in a vacant field near her home. There was something girlish and
charming about her.

Shirley Temple Black and Teresa Falaschi. Los Angeles, 1988
She asked her grand-daughter, Teresa, to join her when I asked her to dance. She
told the child, 'I hope you haven't forgotten the steps
Granny showed you.'

Joe Namath, Margaux Hemingway and Cary Grant. San Francisco, 1976
On the road, sometimes the only place for a studio is my hotel bedroom.
Football hero Namath, model Hemingway and movie star Grant were an
unlikely threesome, but they were together promoting a men's fragrance. *People*
magazine wanted a cover of the three of them and it was the only time they
would all be together.

Priscilla Presley. Memphis, Tennessee, 1987.
We were getting close to Elvis's bedroom. When I asked her to pose inside, this
was her reply.

Robert Plant. Memphis, Tennessee, 1987
Life planned a tribute to Elvis on the tenth anniversary of his death. Plant, who
travelled from London to be photographed at Graceland, was overwhelmed when
he first set foot in the foyer. He had to leave and go stand by a tree.

Billy Joel. Memphis, Tennessee, 1987
At Elvis's golden grand piano, a gift from Priscilla, Joel pounded out
'Heartbreak Hotel'. By the time Joel was in the fourth grade, he told me, he had
begun to imitate his idol in school talent-shows.

Ron Wood. Memphis, Tennessee, 1987
Rolling Stone Wood posed in front of the 1955 pink Cadillac that Elvis gave his
mother. All of the performers who came to Graceland for the *Life* tribute said
they owed their careers to Presley.

Laura Ashley. Rhydoldog Estate, Wales, 1983
She reminded me of a character from an Agatha Christie novel. I wanted the picture to look like a schoolteacher out for a picnic with her girls.

Jane Pauley. New York, 1989
After thirteen years on the *Today Show*, she had just
announced her resignation. At five in the morning,
with her usual cup of black coffee, as the sun rose over
Central Park, she stood by the window. She was
bewildered as to why *Life* wanted her for the cover.
This was the first picture taken in her home. She keeps
her family life separate from her public life.

**Mohammad Reza Pahlavi, Shah of Iran.
Noshahr, Iran, 1978**

The Shah wanted to show me the view from his
window and kept calling me over. Not moving, I told
him if he would ask his Great Dane guard dog, Beno,
to get his foot off my foot I would be able to cross the
room. Laughing, he told me Beno had no sense of
humour. When called off Beno sat by his master's side.

Mrs Ethel Kennedy and Family. McLean, Virginia, 1988
On the anniversary of Bobby Kennedy's birthday, his family and friends gathered
at the family home, Hickory Hill. Most of them were celebrating and
remembering a father they hardly knew. Bobby Kennedy was one of those people
you were fortunate to touch in your travels. It's hard to believe that all this time
has passed. Mrs Kennedy stands with Robert Jr, holding his son, Robert II, and
several of her grandchildren beneath a portrait of Bobby.

Mrs Barbara Bush. Washington DC, 1989
Checking the preparations for a State dinner in the White House, her favourite
King Charles spaniel followed her everywhere. Mrs Bush had just recovered
from thyroid surgery and was beginning to return to the hectic schedule
she must maintain.

Caroline and John Kennedy, Jr. Boston, Massachusetts, 1984
For a story on all the presidents' children, Caroline and John Jr sat on the lawn
behind the John F. Kennedy Library. They were posing for the first time
since childhood. Both asked what they should do, saying they had never
done this before.

Tessa and Wendy Benson. Oxford, 1989
No book would ever be complete without a picture of my children.

Robin Givens. Los Angeles, 1988
I had read about the carry-on in her divorce from Mike Tyson, but I must say I
found her to be charming, articulate and beautiful. People are never what you
expect. When a person tells me I'm going to love photographing someone,
then instinctively I know I will have problems. With Robin Givens it
was the opposite.

Brooke Shields. New York, 1978
Tired of seeing her made to be what she was not, I wanted to show what I
had seen – a thirteen-year-old capable of clowning around like the youngster
she was.

Fernando Bujones. New York, 1985
While photographing ballet dancer Bujones on the beach, I liked the way the
water seemed to dance around his feet. Earlier he had fun with his two children
in his backyard, playing ball with them, showing them ballet steps.

Farrah Fawcett. New York, 1981
I had photographed her before, when she first came to Hollywood. She was in
better shape now – tiny and fit. She was polite but firm in knowing how she
wanted to look, so while the hairdresser and make-up person sat watching, she
did her own hair and make-up for the cover portrait for *People*.

Lee Radziwill and Herbert Ross. New York, 1988
They had just recently married. When I came into her living-room she casually
sat on the arm of the sofa and asked what I wanted her to do. It was spontaneous
and I said just sit where you are.

Brandon and Lilly Tartikoff. Los Angeles, 1990
President of the NBC television network, Brandon Tartikoff and his wife, Lilly,
formerly a dancer with the New York City Ballet, stand in front of their
Coldwater Canyon home. She has a fun-loving and zany personality and I
suggested she put on her ballet slippers and have some fun. They have every
reason to celebrate, for he took NBC from last to first place in the television
ratings with hits like *The Cosby Show* and *Cheers*.

Julianne Phillips.
Manhattan Beach, California, 1987
She told me she got more love from her dog than from
her husband, rock star Bruce Springsteen. Six months
later they were divorced.

Kelly McGillis. Los Angeles, 1988
She was playing on the beach with her dog, throwing a ball for him to fetch, and
she had got sand all over herself. She was pleasant and likeable, and I had a good
time photographing her.

Roman Polanski. Seychelles, 1976
While doing an assignment for French *Vogue* on pirates, I thought of burying
Roman up to his neck in the sand. He got a bit frightened, a bit apprehensive,
when the tide came in and he discovered he couldn't get out without my help.

Diana Vreeland. New York, 1983
While preparing for an exhibit for the Costume
Institute of the Metropolitan Museum of Art, she sat
down among the mannequins. Mrs Vreeland had a
great sense of drama and style.

122

Donald Trump. New York, 1988
The canvas backdrop was painted to represent his golden empire – Trump
Tower, Wollman skating rink – which he renovated in months, doing what the
city hadn't been able to do in years. We were in his New York office and I pulled
back to show where we were.

Jean Harris. Bedford Hills Correctional Facility, New York, 1983
Former headmistress of the prestigious Madeira School in Virginia, now in
prison for killing her lover, diet specialist Dr Herman Tarnower, she works in
the prison day-care centre teaching the children of other inmates. Before I saw
her, one of the security guards said, 'I've seen all kinds come through here, and I
mean all kinds, but I'll tell you that this woman is a genuine person, a real lady.'

Halston. New York, 1978

Halston was larger than life. In the many times I photographed him, he never wasted my time – one of those celebrities who really wanted to oblige. I always knew with Halston I would not come back empty-handed. He knew his image was that of glamorous fashion designer and he loved it. This was the last photograph I took of him – running up the stairs of his townhouse.

127

Frank Moschino. Milan, 1987
Moschino thinks fashion should be fun. His witty sense of humour is evident in
the clothes he designs. He is the opposite of what he looks like on first meeting
– a quiet man who could be a sparring partner for a boxer.

Giorgio Armani. Milan, 1987
What I find interesting about the very talented and the very busy is that they
will always find a moment. Nothing is too much for them. This picture was
taken right in the middle of Armani designing his Spring Collection, with
women with swatches of cloth running around and telephones ringing
constantly. Amid seeming chaos he stopped everything to give me
half-hour of his time.

Jessye Norman. Aix-en-Provence, 1985
The great strength and energy of the internationally renowned opera star Jessye
Norman come across to the audience when she sings. She told me that slaves
sang not so much because they were happy, but because they were sad.

Galanos. Los Angeles, 1985
Favourite fashion designer of Nancy Reagan and her group of friends, he brought
out all the fitting forms of his famous clients for the photograph.

Elliott Roosevelt and wife, Patty. Indian Wells, California, 1984
I was struck by his resemblance to his famous father, in profile and in manner.

Francis Grover Cleveland. Tamworth, New Hampshire, 1984
While his father was President, the Statue of Liberty was dedicated and
Geronimo went on the warpath. Born after his father left office, he has never been
in the White House and doesn't seem to care. Eighty-one-year-old Francis
Cleveland rehearses for the comedy, *Harvey*, about a man and his imaginary
rabbit. An actor who helped found a theatre group in 1931 near where he lives,
he still performs in its productions.

Sukhreet Gabel and her mother, Hortense. New York, 1988
At the time Sukhreet was testifying against her mother in an investigation.
It seems former Miss America and New York Cultural Affairs Commissioner
Bess Myerson gave Sukhreet a job on the city payroll when Andy Capasso
(Myerson's boyfriend) was divorcing and Judge Gabel was hearing the case in
which alimony would be set.

Bunker Hunt. Dallas, 1980
He had reportedly tried to corner the market in silver and *Life* sent me, with a
reporter, to try to get the story. He said, 'Yes, if I can edit the text.'
Of course *Life* would not agree, but before leaving, I asked to take
one quick picture in his office.

Jimmy Breslin. Queens, New York, 1988
He is New York's number one newspaper columnist. He's that because he takes
the side of the little man, the dissatisfied, and he loves it. The people he writes
about come from all walks of life, usually from the boroughs of Brooklyn and
Queens. He's not afraid to take a shot at any official he feels deserves it.

Lee Iacocca and his mother, Antoinette. Allentown, Pennsylvania, 1986
The Chrysler chief made the mistake of telling me that his mother was still the
boss so I asked her to give him a piece of her mind. She launched into an old
reprimand from his childhood which made him smile.

King Juan Carlos. Madrid, 1985
After photographing the King and Queen and their family, the King showed me his dogs. I must have been thirty yards away when he picked up two puppies by the scruff of the neck and put them back into their pen. I went back over to the pen and left the door open. Of course the dogs ran out. He looked at me as if to ask why I left the door open. He naturally had to go and get them again. This time I didn't have to run thirty yards to get the picture.

138

Donna Karan. New York, 1988
America's top woman fashion designer is always on the
run. She leaves her make-up for the limousine on the
way to work, and she talks incessantly on the phone at
the same time. She's very happy with her success.

Michael Jackson. Philadelphia, 1984
On stage the tenseness, the nervous energy, show, but
off stage Michael is very, very quiet and shy. He liked
my jacket, an English tweed·riding jacket, which I gave
him. He seemed pleased and immediately put it on.

143

Jacqueline Bissett. Salvador, Brazil, 1989
She's always a good sport and I've known her for a long time. Nothing is too
much trouble in helping you to get a good picture.

Marcello Mastroianni. Rome, 1987

I'd never seen anyone smoke so many cigarettes. Before one was half-finished, he had another ready to go. At the time he was doing *Uncle Vanya* on stage in Rome. The first film I ever saw him in was *La Dolce Vita* – one of the best films I've ever seen. He was exactly as I thought he would be, a man who is completely his own boss.

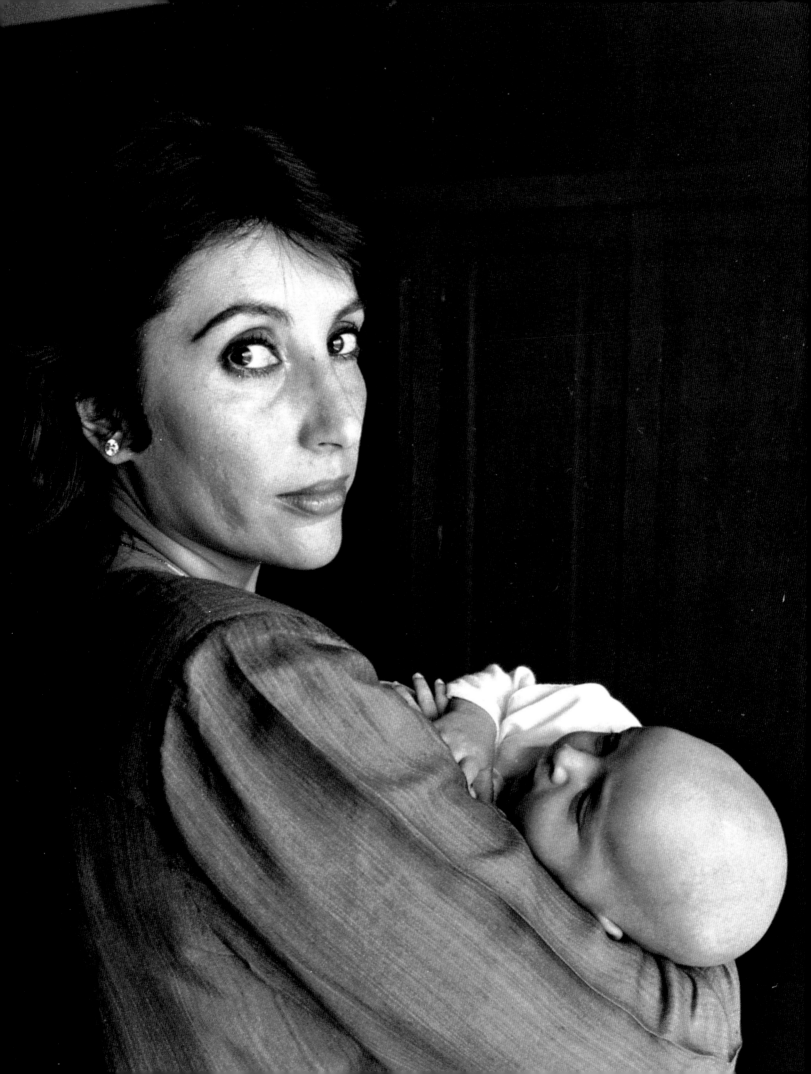

President Benazir Bhutto. Karachi, Pakistan, 1988
After travelling all the way to Karachi I was told she was off in the north
campaigning for the presidency and wouldn't be back for three weeks. The
thought of waiting three weeks was not something I relished. I hung up the
phone, looked out of my hotel window and the phone rang again. There had
been a mistake and my appointment was for one o'clock that day. In Pakistan it's
safe to say women come second, but no one told Benazir Bhutto that. She gives
precise orders to her staff; she is totally in charge.

Priscilla and Navarone Presley. Beverly Hills, 1988
Priscilla Presley and her eleven-month-old son, Navarone, in a park near their
home. She said that Navarone had been a wonderful learning experience for Lisa
Marie, her daughter by Elvis, to see how a baby dominates a mother's life.

Arnold Schwarzenegger. Los Angeles, 1985
In the pool of his Los Angeles home, Schwarzenegger shows off the body that has
made him a star. He said he'd be sick in the head if he didn't appreciate the
life he's been given.

Dolly Parton. Nashville, Tennessee, 1976
She was looking into a full-length mirror and said she would be ready in a
minute. I answered, just keep doing what you are doing. It was a completely
spontaneous picture and by far the most natural one I took that day.

Jack Nicholson and Anjelica Huston. New York, 1985
They were both in *Prizzi's Honor* and posed for the cover of *People* to publicise the
film. He obliged strictly for her, to help her career. She was very quick-witted.
Nicholson, in my mind, is probably America's foremost actor today.

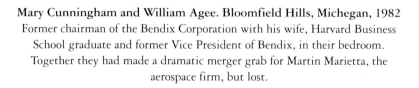

Mary Cunningham and William Agee. Bloomfield Hills, Michegan, 1982
Former chairman of the Bendix Corporation with his wife, Harvard Business
School graduate and former Vice President of Bendix, in their bedroom.
Together they had made a dramatic merger grab for Martin Marietta, the
aerospace firm, but lost.

George Burns. Hollywood, 1988

George Burns visits his wife, Gracie, every week. He sits there in the mausoleum and talks to her for a while, telling her what he has been doing. He touches the stone and, on tiptoe, kisses it before he leaves. He told me she was in good company with Jeanette MacDonald and Ramon Navarro in nearby vaults to talk to at night when he's not there.

153

Princess Grace. Paris, 1982
This was one of the last photographs to be taken of her. She was a woman who
loved to be photographed. That day she was waiting, in her Paris apartment, for
her daughter, Stephanie, to arrive home from school.

Prince Rainier. Monte Carlo, Monaco, 1989
A very quiet, refined man. There is a look of sadness and loneliness about him.
He said the portrait on the wall was just how he remembers her.

Bobby Fischer. Reykjavik, Iceland, 1972
While playing for the World Chess Championship
against Boris Spassky, he was literally a recluse.
Isolating himself from everyone, including his own
mother, he was afraid his telephone was being tapped
by the Russians and he kept his door tightly locked.
Having a horse kiss him seemed to fit in with the
idiosyncrasies of his personality. He asked me
afterwards if the horse would give him blood poisoning
– that question from a genius who could think twenty-
five moves ahead in a game of chess.

John Mitchell. New York, 1974

Attorney General Mitchell had been acquitted of conspiracy in the Vesco case in
his first Watergate trial – and he was jubilant. After everyone else from the press
had gone, he invited me into his hotel suite. When he heard I was Scottish, he
sang the songs of Harry Lauder, an old-time Scottish vaudeville comedian.

President and Mrs Richard Nixon.
The White House, Washington DC, 1974

I always knew Pat Nixon was an emotional person, not as cold as the press had
made her out to be when they dubbed her 'plastic Pat'. So I was ready for her
tear during the President's farewell speech to his staff on his last day in office.

Mayor Ed Koch. New York, 1989
The lonely bachelor at home in Gracie Mansion with a
solitary porcelain rabbit was fighting for his political
life. The polls gave him no chance of winning
re-election – and win he didn't, but it was close.

Donald and Ivana Trump. New York, 1988
People magazine wanted me to get a photograph at
their home in Connecticut, but with both their busy
schedules there wasn't time. We photographed their
New York bedroom instead. Donald likes to talk about
his health and his work-out schedule. I like him. He is
good for our business.

J. Paul Getty. London, 1974

In his London mansion shortly before he died, he
talked about how daffodils were his favourite flower,
how they were harbingers of spring. Only later did I
recall the poignancy of his remarks that day. When I
told him I had attended a gala party years before at his
home he said he was thinking of having another one.

But the party never came about.

Truman Capote. New York, 1976
He was very bright and had an uncanny way of reading your mind. A very tough little man. He always had an amusing story to tell – he made me laugh.

Truman Capote. Long Island, 1984
Truman was the most delightful, most melancholic person I have ever met. Months before he died, he took me to the beach at his summer home where he had scampered as a young man.

INDEX